Let Freedom Ring

Miles Standish

Colonial Leader

by Barbara Witteman

Consultant:
Len Travers
Assistant Professor
University of Massachusetts Dartmouth
North Dartmouth, Massachusetts

Capstone
press
Mankato, Minnesota

Capstone Press
151 Good Counsel Drive • P.O. Box 669 • Mankato, Minnesota 56002
http://www.capstonepress.com

Library of Congress Cataloging-in-Publication Data
Witteman, Barbara.
    Miles Standish: colonial leader / by Barbara Witteman.
       p. cm.—(Let freedom ring)
    Summary: A biography of Miles Standish, military soldier and leader of
the Plymouth Colony, who sailed aboard the *Mayflower* to help protect the
Pilgrims and their settlement in North America.
    Includes bibliographical references and index.
    ISBN 0-7368-2457-X (hardcover)
    ISBN 0-7368-4485-6 (paperback)
    1. Standish, Myles, 1584?–1656—Juvenile literature. 2. Pilgrims (New Plymouth
Colony)—Juvenile literature. 3. Soldiers—Massachusetts—Biography—Juvenile literature.
4. Massachusetts—History—New Plymouth, 1620–1691—Biography—Juvenile literature.
[1. Standish, Myles, 1584?–1656. 2. Soldiers. 3. Pilgrims (New Plymouth Colony)]
I. Title. II. Series.
F68.S87W58 2004
974.4'01'092—dc22   2003013915

Editorial Credits
Donald Lemke, editor; Kia Adams, series designer; Enoch Peterson, book designer
    and illustrator; Jo Miller and Wanda Winch, photo researchers; Eric Kudalis,
    product planning editor

Photo Credits
Bridgeman Art Library/Harris Museum and Art Gallery, Preston, Lancashire, UK, 41
Cape Ann Historical Museum, Gloucester, Massachusetts, 39
Capstone Press Archives, 35
Corbis/Bettmann, 7, 15, 17; Charles Philip, 9
Getty Images Inc./Hulton/Archive, cover; Time Life Pictures, 13
The Granger Collection, New York, 18, 24
North Wind Picture Archives, 5, 11, 21, 23, 31, 33, 36, 42, 43
Photri-Microstock, 16
Stock Montage Inc., 27

The author dedicates this book to Karen, a *Mayflower* descendent.

1   2   3   4   5   6   09   08   07   06   05   04

Table of Contents

Chapter One

Plymouth Soldier

Miles Standish wanted to protect the settlers of Plymouth Colony. He knew that Massachuset Indians were planning an attack on a nearby settlement. This Indian group wanted to take back their land from the settlers. Some of them wanted to kill the **Pilgrims**.

In March 1623, Standish met with the leaders of the Massachuset, including Pecksuot. Pecksuot was much bigger and taller than Standish. Pecksuot bragged that he was a man of great strength and courage. He threatened Standish and called him a little man.

Standish was short and stocky, but he had a big temper. The next day, Standish and the Massachuset Indians met again. Suddenly, Standish attacked Pecksuot and snatched his knife from him. Then, Standish stabbed and killed Pecksuot.

In 1623, Miles Standish, in a blue coat, and other Pilgrims of Plymouth Colony fought several Massachuset Indian leaders.

Standish had fought hard to protect the colony. After the fight, other American Indian groups were scared. They came to Plymouth to ask for peace treaties.

Pilgrims and the American Indians

When the Pilgrims first arrived in North America, thousands of Indians were already living in the area. Many settlers believed they had a right to build homes on the land. They often took land and food without paying for it. These actions upset American Indians and started many conflicts.

Standish came to North America to help protect the colonists from these conflicts. He trained the men at Plymouth and tried to fight only when necessary. Standish also learned several American Indian languages. He tried to develop peaceful relations with many Indian groups, such as the Wampanoag.

The Pilgrims welcomed Massasoit, a Wampanoag leader, into Plymouth Colony. The settlers formed peaceful relations with members of the Wampanoag.

Chapter Two

Early Life

In 1584, Miles Standish was born in Ellenbane, a town on the Isle of Man. His parents died when he was young. As an **orphan**, Standish learned to be confident and brave. He also became physically strong. These qualities would help Standish become a successful soldier.

In 1601, Standish joined the English army. During this time, Queen Elizabeth I of England was sending troops to Holland to help the Dutch. The Dutch were fighting against the Spanish army.

While in Holland, Standish met a group of Separatists from England. The Separatists were people who fled from England in order to worship freely.

In Holland, the Separatists could worship as they pleased. But their children were **influenced** by Dutch customs, such as dancing.

The Isle of Man is Miles Standish's birthplace. This small island is located off the northwest coast of England.

The Separatists

In 1509, King Henry VIII decided to start his own church called the Church of England. The king required everyone in England to attend this church. People could be punished for not belonging to the Church of England.

Some people did not believe in everything that the Church of England taught. These people were called Puritans. Some Puritans thought they could change the church. Others wanted to completely break away from the Church of England. They wanted to form their own religion. These people were called Separatists. Some Separatists moved to Holland, where they could worship freely.

Separatists did not allow dancing. The Separatists wanted to move to a place where their children would not be influenced by others. They decided to move to North America.

John Robinson was a Separatist minister and a friend of Standish. Robinson had heard stories about troubles with American Indians in North America.

Robinson believed his people needed a leader with military training. He asked Standish to come to North America and help protect the settlers. Standish and his wife, Rose, agreed to go. Standish was 36 years old.

In 1620, many people in Europe left family and friends for North America. Some of these groups rowed small boats to reach ships anchored offshore.

Chapter Three

Coming to America

The Separatists bought a ship named the *Speedwell*. They sailed to England where more people and another ship called the *Mayflower* joined them. In August 1620, the *Speedwell* and the *Mayflower* planned to leave for North America.

Unfortunately, the *Speedwell* started to leak. The ship could not be fixed. The two ships had to return to England. In September 1620, the *Mayflower* set sail alone. The ship had 102 passengers, including Standish and his wife. They planned to land in the area of present-day Virginia.

The Pilgrims

About half of the passengers on the *Mayflower* were Separatists. The other half were people who hoped to find riches in North America. These people became known as "Strangers."

In September 1620, Standish and other passengers set sail for North America aboard the *Mayflower*.

Standish and Rose were Strangers. Standish was a friend of the Separatists, but he was not a member of their church. The Separatists hoped that some of the Strangers would join their faith.

The two groups did not share the same religion, but they did share a common goal. The Separatists and the Strangers hoped for a better life in North America. Together these groups became known as the Pilgrims.

The New World

After sailing for more than 60 days, the Pilgrims finally sighted land. In November 1620, the *Mayflower* dropped anchor off what is now the coast of Massachusetts. This spot was north of the area where they had planned to land.

Before the Pilgrims went ashore, most men on the ship signed the Mayflower Compact. Those who signed the **document** agreed to obey the newly elected officials. John Carver was elected the first governor. This was the first English **democratic** election to take place in North America.

In November 1620, Standish and other men aboard the *Mayflower* signed the Mayflower Compact.

The Mayflower Compact

Before going ashore, 41 men aboard the *Mayflower* signed the Mayflower Compact. This document described the Pilgrims' plan to establish a colony in North America. It also set up a government with laws to help the colony succeed. The beginning of this historical document is printed below.

IN THE NAME OF GOD, AMEN. We, whose names are underwritten, the Loyal Subjects of our dread Sovereign Lord King James, by the Grace of God, of Great Britain, France, and Ireland, King, Defender of the Faith, etc. Having undertaken for the Glory of God, and Advancement of the Christian Faith, and the Honour of our King and Country, a Voyage to plant the first Colony in the northern Parts of Virginia; Do by these Presents, solemnly and mutually, in the Presence of God and one another, covenant and combine ourselves together into a civil Body Politick, for our better Ordering and Preservation, and Furtherance of the Ends aforesaid: And by Virtue hereof do enact, constitute, and frame, such just and equal Laws, Ordinances, Acts, Constitutions, and Officers . . .

Exploration and Settlement

Soon, Standish and 15 other men went ashore. They needed to explore the land and find a good place to live. The men were disappointed. They only found sandy soil and could not find fresh water. Until Standish and the other men could find better land, the passengers had to stay on the *Mayflower*.

The *Mayflower* anchored off the coast of present-day Massachusetts. Standish and other men rowed to shore to find fresh water.

Standish and his men continued to explore. While exploring the land, they saw American Indians for the first time. The Pilgrims found food stored by the Indians. They took it. The men also found American Indian graves, which they robbed.

While exploring the area of Plymouth, the Pilgrims found corn stored by American Indians. They took these supplies without asking.

Did You Know?

A plaque in Provincetown, Massachusetts, honors the 300th anniversary of the exploration of Standish and 15 other Pilgrims. It marks the spot where the Pilgrims spent their second night on American soil on November 16, 1620.

Standish led three exploration trips while looking for a good place to live. On the third trip, Standish and his men were surprised by an Indian attack. Some American Indians wanted to get even for the stolen corn and the robbed graves. Many of the Pilgrims were not prepared. Luckily, their **muskets** frightened most of the American Indians away. But one Indian kept shooting arrows. Standish fired his musket at a tree. Flying bark startled the man, who ran into the woods. Although no one was hurt, the attack made the settlers more fearful of American Indians.

Chapter Four

Plymouth Colony

*I*n December 1620, the Pilgrims finally found a place with fresh water. The site was 40 miles (64 kilometers) south of what is now Boston, Massachusetts. The area was later named Plymouth Colony.

Soon, the Pilgrims started building shelters in the new colony. They built a common house for meetings and homes to live in. Standish and Rose built their home at the base of a hill overlooking Plymouth. A fort was later built on the top of the hill. In case of an attack, Standish could quickly climb the hill to the fort. The Pilgrims called the area Fort Hill.

The Great Sickness

By January 1621, most of the settlers in Plymouth Colony were ill. This illness became known as the "Great Sickness."

During the first year, the Pilgrims worked hard to build shelter
for everyone in Plymouth Colony.

The Words of a Pilgrim

"In ye time of most distress there was but 6 or 7 sound persons; who to their great comendations, be it spoken, spared no pains, night nor day, but with abundance of love, and [hazard] of their owne health, fetched them wood, made them fires, drest them meat, made their beds, washed there…cloaks, cloathed and uncloathed them, in a word did all ye homly and necessarie offices for them…and all this willingly and cherfully…"

—William Bradford, *History of Plymouth Plantation*, describing the help Standish and others gave to the sick Pilgrims during the "Great Sickness"

On January 29, 1621, Rose became one of the first settlers to die from the illness. Standish was one of only seven people not to become sick. He nursed the sick Pilgrims, buried the dead, and kept a watchful eye out for Indians.

In February 1621, Standish was named the military commander of Plymouth. In two days, he set up a defense system. Five cannons were brought ashore from the *Mayflower*. The Pilgrims placed the cannons on Fort Hill. Standish assigned the men duty posts and prepared them for battle.

American Indian Visitors

In March 1621, an Abenaki Indian walked into Plymouth. His name was Samoset. He spoke to the Pilgrims in English. After spending the night, Samoset left. He promised to return.

In March 1621, Samoset walked into Plymouth Colony. He was the first American Indian to make friendly contact with the Pilgrims.

When Samoset returned a few days later, he brought a Patuxet Indian named Squanto and two other Indian men. The men had a message from Massasoit, a leader of the Wampanoag. The chief wanted to make a friendly visit to Plymouth.

Squanto served as a guide for Standish and other settlers in Plymouth Colony.

Squanto

Tisquantum, called Squanto by the Pilgrims, was a Patuxet Indian. He lived in the area of Plymouth. In 1614, Captain Thomas Hunt captured Squanto and several other American Indians. Hunt took the Indians to Spain and tried to sell them as slaves.

In 1619, Squanto sailed back to North America. Unfortunately, every member of Squanto's village had been killed by disease. Squanto went to Massasoit and asked to live with the Wampanoag. Massasoit granted this request.

During his travels, Squanto had learned how to speak English. After returning to North America, he served as an interpreter and guide for the Pilgrims. He showed them how to plant corn, where to fish, and how to trade. His skills helped the Pilgrims survive. In December 1622, Squanto died of a fever.

Several days later, Massasoit came to Plymouth. Standish and his men greeted the Wampanoag chief. They welcomed the chief and his men into the settlement. Squanto served as an **interpreter**.

He helped the Pilgrims and American Indians talk to each other. The two groups agreed to a peace treaty. This treaty lasted for more than 50 years.

Conflicts with American Indians

Standish knew that some American Indians wanted the Pilgrims to leave. He had the Pilgrims build a log wall around Plymouth for added safety. This wall was almost 8 feet (2.4 meters) tall and a half-mile (.8 kilometer) long. The gates were protected by guards.

Corbitant was a member of Massasoit's tribe. He disagreed with Massasoit and the peace treaty. Corbitant did not like the English. In August 1621, he tried to get other American Indians to **revolt** against Massasoit. Corbitant captured Squanto and his friend Hobomak. Somehow, Hobomak managed to escape and return to Plymouth. He told the Pilgrims that Squanto was probably dead.

During a meeting in 1621, Massasoit offered a peace pipe to Governor Carver of Plymouth Colony. The Pilgrims and the Wampanoag agreed to a peace treaty, which lasted more than 50 years.

Standish and 10 other men went to capture Corbitant. Hobomak served as their guide. On August 14, 1621, Standish surprised the American Indians at Corbitant's camp. He discovered that Corbitant and his men had escaped. Standish also found Squanto alive and unhurt.

Wessagusett

As new settlers arrived in North America, more problems started with American Indians. In 1622, Thomas Weston from England founded Wessagusett. This settlement was located near Plymouth Colony, in the area of present-day Weymouth, Massachusetts. The men at Wessagusett stole food from the American Indians and cheated them in trade. This behavior put the settlers of Wessagusett in danger. The Pilgrims were also in danger because of their close location to Weston's settlement.

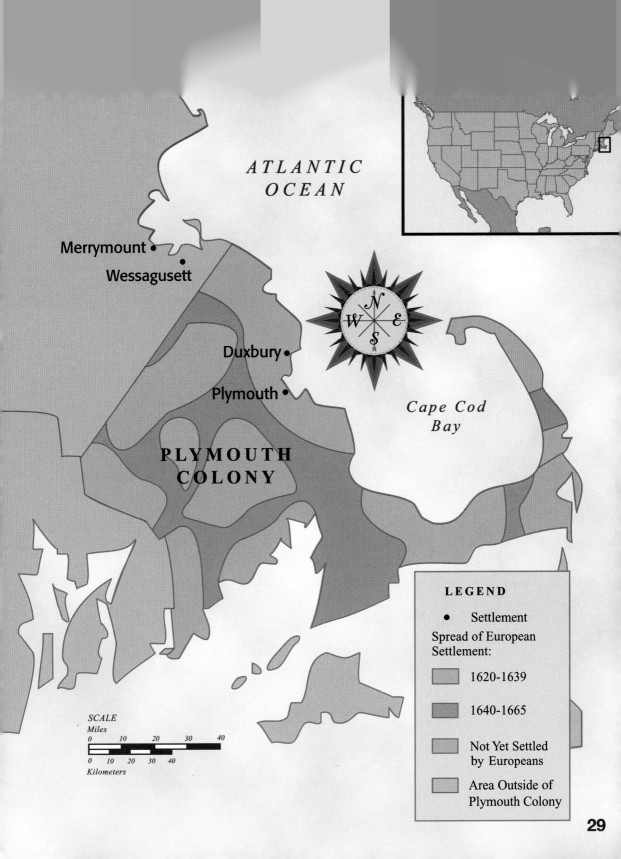

ATLANTIC
OCEAN

Merrymount •
Wessagusett •

Duxbury •

Plymouth •

Cape Cod
Bay

**PLYMOUTH
COLONY**

LEGEND

• Settlement

Spread of European
Settlement:

1620-1639

1640-1665

Not Yet Settled
by Europeans

Area Outside of
Plymouth Colony

SCALE
Miles
0   10   20   30   40

0   10   20   30   40
Kilometers

In March 1623, Massasoit told the Pilgrims that the Massachuset Indians planned to destroy Wessagusett. Standish took some men and left for Weston's settlement. He offered these settlers the protection of Plymouth soldiers.

While in Wessagusett, Standish met with leaders of the Massachuset, including Pecksuot, Wituwamet, and Wituwamet's brother. During the meeting, Pecksuot threatened Standish and called him a little man. Standish became angry and started a fight with the Massachuset leader. While they were fighting, Standish took Pecksuot's knife from him. He stabbed Pecksuot. The Pilgrims also killed Wituwamet. Wituwamet's brother was captured and later hanged for planning to destroy Wessagusett.

Standish cut off Wituwamet's head. He took it to Plymouth and displayed it on a pole at the fort. Many American Indians took this as a warning.

They knew that Standish was small in size but he would fight hard. Many tribes decided that peace was better than fighting. Some of them came to Plymouth to sign peace treaties with the Pilgrims.

Standish and other Pilgrims returned to Plymouth Colony after defeating the leaders of the Massachuset Indians.

Chapter Five

New Beginnings

In July 1623, more ships carrying new settlers arrived at Plymouth. A woman named Barbara was on one of these ships. Some historians believe that Barbara was the sister of Standish's first wife. Standish probably knew Barbara before she came to North America. Soon after she arrived, Standish and Barbara were married. Eventually, the couple had six sons and one daughter.

The Pilgrims' Debt

The Pilgrims had borrowed money from English businessmen to come to America. They needed to repay this debt. The Pilgrims sent ships loaded with furs and fish to England. Unfortunately, pirates captured some of these ships and stole the cargo. The Pilgrims needed one of their leaders to go to London and help solve their debt problems.

While living in Plymouth Colony, Standish was more than
a military leader. He also supported a family and helped the
colony with business affairs.

In 1625, Standish traveled to London. He and several other leaders from Plymouth Colony decided to repay the debt. Standish and the other leaders became known as **undertakers**. The undertakers made decisions about Plymouth's business affairs. The debt was finally paid off in 1648.

Merrymount

One of the people Standish asked for help in London was Sir Ferdinando Gorges. Gorges refused to help the Pilgrims with their loan. Instead, he helped Captain Wollaston and Thomas Morton start Mount Wollaston in 1626. This settlement was just north of present-day Quincy, Massachusetts. It competed with Plymouth for trade with American Indians in the area.

In 1628, Morton became the leader of Mount Wollaston. He renamed it Merrymount. The men at Merrymount did not have rules. They drank alcohol and danced. Morton sold guns to American Indians and showed them how to use them. The Pilgrims asked Morton to stop selling guns, but he refused.

Standish and eight men went to Merrymount. Morton did not like Standish and called him Captain Shrimp. Morton rushed at Standish to attack him.

Thomas Morton and other settlers at Merrymount drank alcohol and traded guns with American Indians.

Standish grabbed Morton by his collar and pulled his gun away. The rest of Morton's group simply watched. Standish and his men brought Morton to Plymouth. They sent him back to England on the next ship leaving the colony.

Duxbury

In 1632, Standish and his family left the Plymouth settlement and helped found a new village just 3 miles (5 kilometers) away. This new settlement

Pilgrim soldiers watched as settlers and American Indians partied at Merrymount. These celebrations upset the leaders of Plymouth Colony.

The Words of Thomas Morton

"...[I] no sooner had set open the door, and issued out, but instantly Captaine Shrimp and the rest of his worthies stepped to [me], laid hold of [my weapons] and had [me] down..."

—Thomas Morton, on being captured by Standish

was named Duxbury. William Brewster, a former Pilgrim governor, was Standish's neighbor. The land that Standish owned was called Captain's Hill. He owned about 150 acres (60 hectares) of land.

Even though he had moved, Standish continued to help Plymouth Colony succeed. Standish served as the military leader of Plymouth and as a governor's assistant for many years. In May 1653, Standish was named deputy governor of Plymouth.

Unfortunately, these years in Duxbury would be the last of Standish's life. On October 3, 1656, he died at his home. Standish was more than 70 years old.

Chapter Six

Remembering Miles Standish

In 1898, workers completed a memorial for Standish. The 110-foot (34-meter) column of granite stands atop Captain's Hill in Duxbury, Massachusetts. A 14-foot (4-meter) statue of the Plymouth Colony leader rests on top of the column. Visitors can climb 125 steps to look at the statue or take in a view of Plymouth Bay.

Plymouth Leader

Standish was an important member of Plymouth Colony. He served as the colony's military leader from 1621 to 1653. Standish was elected to several political posts, including assistant governor. He also served as **treasurer** for five years, from 1644 to 1649.

During the late 1800s, workers sculpted a 14-foot (4-meter) statue of Miles Standish. Today, the statue overlooks Plymouth Bay.

The Courtship of Miles Standish

Henry Wadsworth Longfellow wrote "The Courtship of Miles Standish" in 1858. The poem describes a love triangle between John Alden, Priscilla Mullins, and Miles Standish. In the poem, Standish wants to ask Priscilla to marry him. Instead, Standish asks John to ask Priscilla for him. Priscilla likes John more than Standish. Eventually, John and Priscilla end up getting married. Although many readers and critics consider the poem a classic, there is no evidence that these events ever happened.

Stern as a soldier might be, but hearty, and placable always,
Not to be laughed at and scorned, because he was little
of stature;
For he was great of heart, magnanimous, courtly, courageous;
Any woman in Plymouth, nay, any woman in England,
Might be happy and proud to be called the wife of
Miles Standish!

—Henry Wadsworth Longfellow

Miles Standish was a soldier at heart. He is remembered for his courage and good judgment. Standish faced challenges quickly and bravely. He was not afraid to fight, but also knew how to solve problems peacefully.

Although small in size, Standish had a big impact on Plymouth Colony. Without his strength and courage, many more of the Pilgrims might have died. Standish was a hero to members of Plymouth Colony.

Longfellow's "The Courtship of Miles Standish" inspired this engraving. In the poem, Standish loses Priscilla Mullins to John Alden. Most of the events in the poem are not true.

TIME LINE

Chronology of Standish's Life

Born in Ellenbane, a town on the Isle of Man

Arrives in the area of Massachusetts aboard the *Mayflower*

Joins the army of Queen Elizabeth I of England

Rose Standish dies

Marries Barbara

| 1584 | 1601 | 1607 | 1620 | 1621 | 1623 |

Historical Events

Settlers from England establish Jamestown Colony, the first permanent white settlement in North America.

Samoset visits Plymouth Colony; Governor Carver and Massasoit, a leader of the Wampanoag, agree to a peace treaty.

The *Mayflower* drops anchor off what is now the coast of Massachusetts.

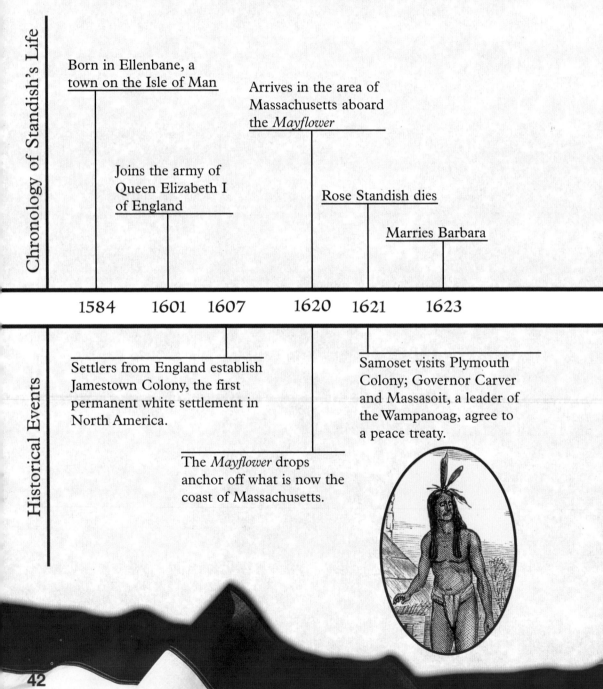

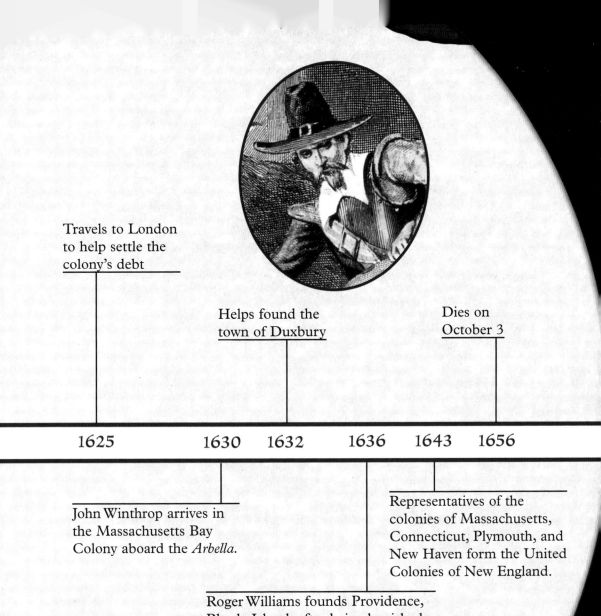

Travels to London
to help settle the
colony's debt

Helps found the
town of Duxbury

Dies on
October 3

| 1625 | 1630 | 1632 | 1636 | 1643 | 1656 |

John Winthrop arrives in
the Massachusetts Bay
Colony aboard the *Arbella*.

Representatives of the
colonies of Massachusetts,
Connecticut, Plymouth, and
New Haven form the United
Colonies of New England.

Roger Williams founds Providence,
Rhode Island, after being banished
from the Massachusetts Bay Colony.

Glossary

democratic (dem-uh-KRAT-ik)—having to do with a government in which people choose their leaders by voting

document (DOK-yuh-muhnt)—a piece of paper containing important information

influence (IN-floo-uhnss)—to have an effect on someone or something

interpreter (in-TUR-prit-uhr)—someone who can tell others what is said in another language

musket (MUHSS-kit)—a gun with a long barrel that was used before the rifle was invented

orphan (OR-fuhn)—a child whose parents are dead

Pilgrims (PIL-gruhmz)—a group of people who left England for religious freedom, came to North America, and founded Plymouth Colony

revolt (ri-VOHLT)—a rebellion against a government or authority

treasurer (TREZH-ur-ur)—the person in charge of the money of a government or company

undertaker (UHN-dur-tay-kur)—a person who takes on the risk and management of a business

Read More

Davis, Kenneth C. *Don't Know Much About the Pilgrims.* New York: HarperCollins, 2002.

Dell, Pamela. *The Plymouth Colony.* Let Freedom Ring. Mankato, Minn.: Capstone Press, 2004.

Erickson, Paul. *Daily Life in the Pilgrim Colony, 1636.* New York: Clarion Books, 2001.

Miller, Susan Martins. *Miles Standish: Plymouth Colony Leader.* Colonial Leaders. Philadelphia: Chelsea House, 1999.

Whitcraft, Melissa. *The Mayflower Compact.* Cornerstones of Freedom. New York: Children's Press, 2003.

Useful Addresses

Myles Standish Monument
Crescent Street
Duxbury, MA 02332
Completed in 1898, this
monument to colonial leader
Miles Standish stands on
Captain's Hill in Duxbury.

Myles Standish State Forest
Cranberry Road
Carver, MA 02330
As the largest publicly owned
recreation area in southern
Massachusetts, Myles Standish
State Forest offers camping,
swimming, biking, and fishing.

Pilgrim Hall Museum
75 Court Street
Plymouth, MA 02360
The Pilgrim Hall Museum has a
variety of Pilgrim possessions and
American Indian artifacts.

Pilgrim Memorial State Park
Water Street
Plymouth, MA 02360
Visited by nearly one million
people each year, Pilgrim
Memorial State Park is home
to Plymouth Rock and a replica
of the *Mayflower*.

Plimoth Plantation
P.O. Box 1620
Plymouth, MA 02362
Plimoth Plantation is a living
history museum that re-creates
life in Plymouth during the 1600s.